"WE CAN ALL RISE TO THE TOP AND HELP OTHER KIDS WHO ARE IN THE NEXT GENERATION AND THE NEXT GENERATION OF PEOPLE WHO WANT TO HELP CHANGE THIS WORLD." —Marley Dias

"IT'S HARD TO HATE SOMEONE YOU KNOW."

—Ziad Ahmed

"YOU HAVE THE ABILITY TO CHANGE YOUR OWN LIFE AND THE WORLD AROUND YOU."

—Jazz Jennings

NO VOICE TOO SMALL

Fourteen Young Americans Making History

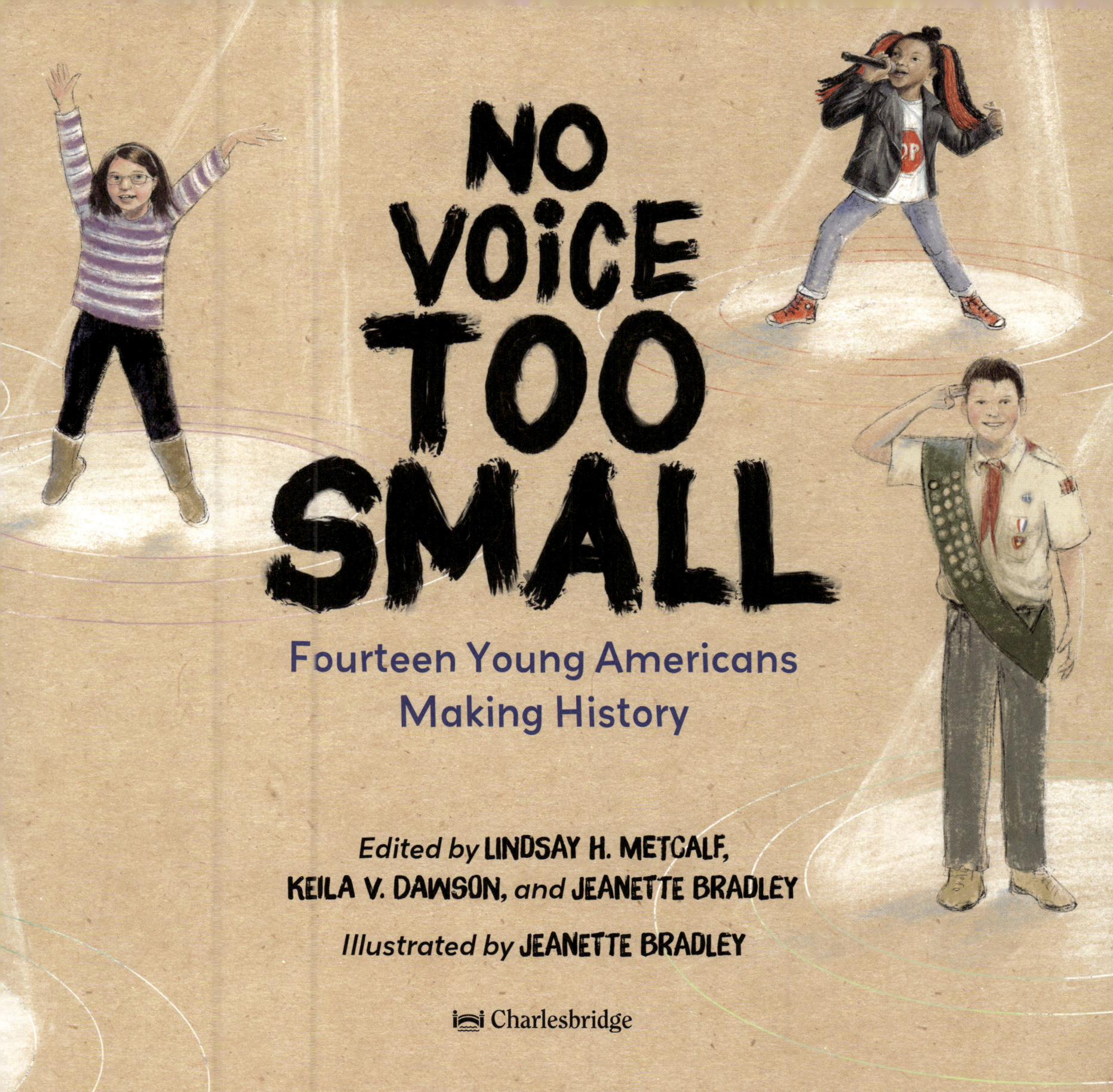

NO VOICE TOO SMALL

Fourteen Young Americans Making History

Edited by **LINDSAY H. METCALF**,
KEILA V. DAWSON, and **JEANETTE BRADLEY**

Illustrated by **JEANETTE BRADLEY**

Charlesbridge

AMPLIFY

A reverso poem by Lindsay H. Metcalf

No voice is too small
to solve a problem
that's big.
A movement
can spark
within you,
your family and friends,
your community,
your country—
within your world.
You see a struggle?
Speak the truth
for others, to
watch
changes
ripple forward.

Ripple forward,
changes.
Watch
for others to
speak the truth—
you see? A struggle
within your world . . .
your country . . .
your community . . .
your family and friends—
within *you*—
can spark
a movement
that's big.
To solve a problem,
no voice is too small.

Meet fourteen young Americans who opened hearts, challenged minds, and changed our world. Each activist inspired a poet who relates to an aspect of the activist's identity. Along the way, find tips for how you, too, can use your voice to make some noise and make a difference.

DJ ANNIE RED: *THE ANTI-BULLYING AMBASSADOR*

A spoken word poem by Charles Waters

This undeniable whirlwind of energy, proudly
representing the People's Republic of Brooklyn,
is stationed at her DJ booth, spinning the wheels
of steel, taking on bullies with her verbal flow,
letting them know their domineering ways have got to go!
Her mission: to heal our fractured hearts one *beat* at a time.

When kids teased Samirah Horton for her low, raspy voice, she used a microphone to speak even louder. At age six, she learned how to work a set of turntables and gave herself the stage name "DJ Annie Red." Samirah raps her song "No You Won't Bully Me" to empower children in her hometown and across the nation.

A catchy tune will stick with people. Set your message to music, and people will hum it all day.

ZIAD AHMED: *DEFY*

A ballad poem by Hena Khan

Talk to me, bring me in,
tell me something new.
Help me see the many ways
I'm just the same as you.

Ask me why, hear me out,
honor what I say.
Together we'll defy the hate
with one small step each day.

Tell your story, raise your voice,
prove how much kids care.
Join with me to make this world
a place we're proud to share.

Growing up Muslim, Ziad Ahmed had been treated unfairly. But he also knew that "it's hard to hate someone you know." So at fourteen, he held face-to-face conversations with almost everyone at his high school. Then he created an online platform where students shared their stories and encouraged others to accept everyone for who they are. His TEDxTeen talk about using personal connections to stop hate has been viewed all over the world.

You can break down stereotypes when you speak out—and when you listen.

JUDY ADAMS: MY NAME IS JUDY

A free verse poem by **Fiona Morris**

I am your friend.
I am your cheerleader.
I make wishes come true . . . just like that.

My gifts I give to all
dreamers who dream big.
My path is my own and my inspiration untamed,
listening for other voices
to speak clear and loud for all to hear.

I listen to the song coming from inside your heart.
And I put inspirations into a jar,
one by one, dime by dime.
While I gather wishes like stars,
we'll make them all come true—to shine.

Judy Adams didn't like to see her mother cry. Her mom wanted to grant a wish to a young man with Down syndrome, but she hadn't raised enough money. So twelve-year-old Judy created Dimes for Down Syndrome, a quest to collect a million dimes. Judy also led others as a high-school cheerleader and gymnastics coach for kids who have special needs. She speaks out about living with Down syndrome.

Small change adds up. Collect coins in a container you decorate yourself. Where will you donate the money?

LEVI DRAHEIM: *THE RISING TIDE*

A free verse poem by G. Neri

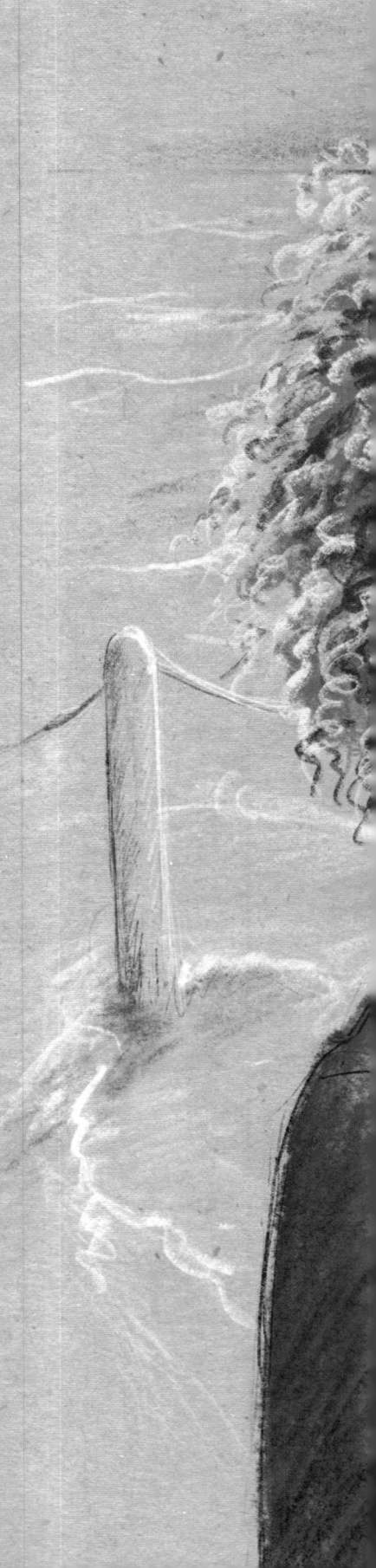

The rain falls.
The wind howls.
The ocean is on the rise,
and we are on the run—
again.

I live on a barrier island
as flat as a Florida pancake,
with the sea at my front door
whispering, *It's time to go!*
And every time we flee,
I wonder:
*How can some people think
this isn't real?*

I keep hearing,
*There's no such thing
as climate change.*
But I know the seas
are rising—
I can see it!

Maybe they don't care
about our future.
But you wanna know
what else can rise up?

Me.
I can become
the sea of change—
a tide that won't stop.
If adults won't stand up
for our future,
then I will.

'Cause somebody's
got to act like a grown-up
around here—
even a kid
like me.

Levi Draheim feared that the seas would swallow his home in Florida before he could grow up and become a marine biologist. In 2015, at age eight, he signed on as the youngest of twenty-one kids who sued the United States government for failing to act on climate change. The lawsuit aimed to force the government to limit the use of fossil fuels and restore a stable climate.

Changing laws can take a long time. Work with friends to help keep you energized.

JAZZ JENNINGS: *FREE*

A free verse poem by S. Bear Bergman

*T*hey gave me the ball and I ran with it,
Jazz says.
As far and as fast as I could.
The tiniest snippet on the soccer field, but
she never felt small.
Do what you want, and be proud of what you can do,
Jazz says.
Even if people might say you're selfish.
That's just what they say about girls
who are confident.
When she got the chance to speak,
she took it and taught us.
Ran trans awareness forward,
down the field, fast and free.
I was a rascal,
Jazz says.
But when the time came, I knew what I could do.
I always knew.

When she was three, Jazz Jennings told her parents that she isn't a boy—she is a girl. Then she proudly told the world. Jazz is many things: public speaker, author, television star, and clothing designer. But first she was an athlete. When her local girls' soccer team banned Jazz from playing, she and her family took the fight to the United States Soccer Federation. Now, thanks to Jazz, transgender soccer players nationwide can play on teams aligned with their genders.

Just be you. Not the you others expect— the you inside. Loving yourself can break down barriers.

CIERRA FIELDS: *WHO'S SHE?*

Two cinquain poems by Traci Sorell

Who's she?
Cherokee girl.
A jingle-dress dancer.
Traditional-arts creator.
Honored.

Who's she?
Youth advocate.
A cancer survivor.
Strong voice for the voiceless victims.
Mighty.

Cierra "Little Water" Fields began sharing information about her experiences with skin cancer when she was twelve. She traveled and spoke out to improve health care in the Cherokee Nation. One day when she was far from home, a man sexually assaulted her. She refused to keep the attack a secret. Telling and writing her story empowered her and gave other Native women courage to speak of their own pain.

The truth is powerful. Revealing it can change attitudes.

NOAH BARNES: MARCHING FOR A CURE

A tanka sequence by **Lindsay H. Metcalf**

Diabetes is:
Insulin shots in public.
Finger pricks. Blood tests.
Enough, Noah Barnes decides.
If there's a cure, I'll find it.

He and Dad pack gear:
GPS, snacks, sunscreen, meds.
Marching like ants, they
inch across the map, Key West
to the opposite corner.

Marble steps lead to
governors, doctors, donors.
He speaks. They promise
to work as hard as his shoes.
Then time for school on the road.

War sites. Trail of Tears.
Tales of survival give hope.
Rockies rise. Shins *scream*.
Sugars drop. Cheese puffs revive.
Forge on, through heat, rain, and pain.

Kid versus disease.
He builds his future by foot—
twenty-two *million*
feet on his coast-to-coast path.
How many more till a cure?

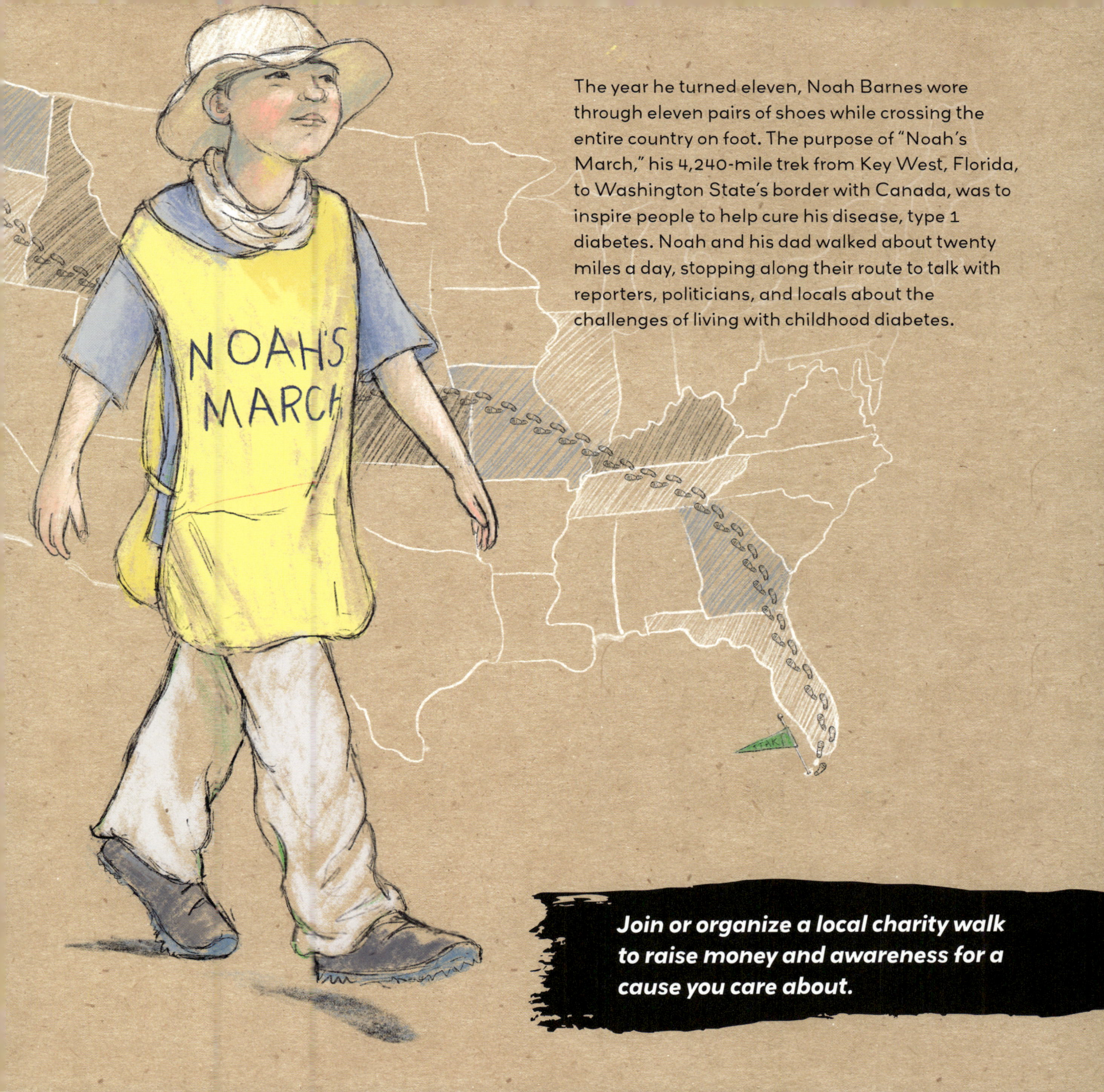

The year he turned eleven, Noah Barnes wore through eleven pairs of shoes while crossing the entire country on foot. The purpose of "Noah's March," his 4,240-mile trek from Key West, Florida, to Washington State's border with Canada, was to inspire people to help cure his disease, type 1 diabetes. Noah and his dad walked about twenty miles a day, stopping along their route to talk with reporters, politicians, and locals about the challenges of living with childhood diabetes.

Join or organize a local charity walk to raise money and awareness for a cause you care about.

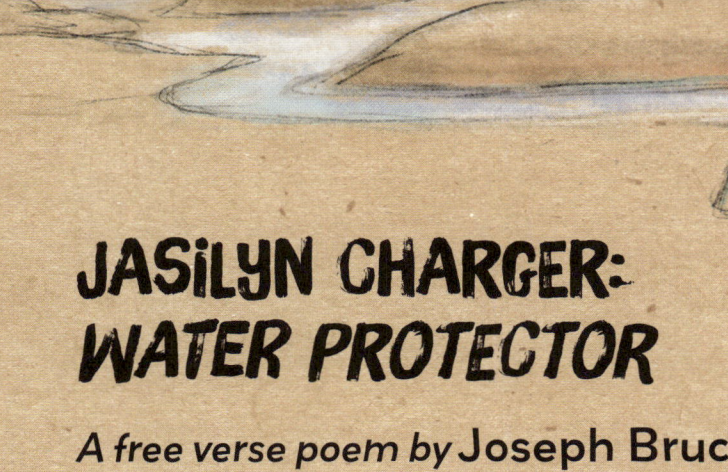

JASILYN CHARGER: WATER PROTECTOR

A free verse poem by **Joseph Bruchac**

We need the river
more than it needs us.
We saw it was time
for us to stand up
against the black snake
that would poison our earth
and destroy our water,
like that snake of despair
that led too many
of our sisters and brothers
to give up on this life.

Ever since the first Europeans
came up the swirling waters
of Mníšoše,
our elders have tried
again and again
to teach them
to respect its blessings.

Now it is our time.
Our new generation
will not give up
this sacred struggle.
It is for our lives,
for all of our relations.

At age nineteen, Jasilyn Charger set up camp with a few friends near Mníšoše (muh-NEE-shoh-sheh), the Lakota name for what colonizers called the Missouri River. They were protesting the construction of a pipeline that threatened to leak oil into the river, which supplies drinking water for the Standing Rock Sioux Tribe as well as millions of people downstream. Jasilyn led two long-distance protest runs, one all the way to Washington, DC. Thousands more water protectors joined the protest on the reservation in North Dakota.

Leaders don't work alone. Join a group or start one to take action.

MARI COPENY: LITTLE MISS FLINT

A concrete poem by
Carole Boston Weatherford

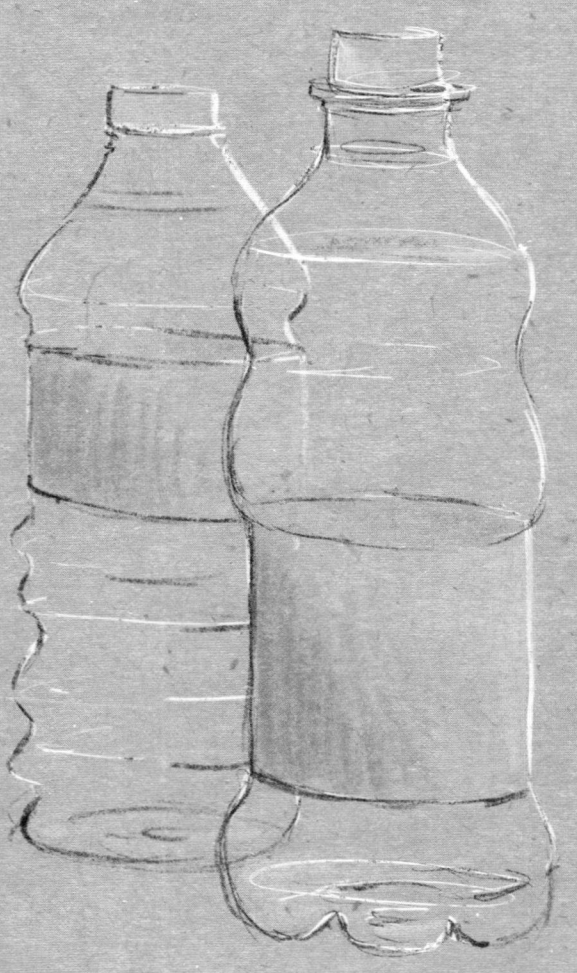

Some
things
can be bottled.
Like water, for example.
Bottled water is a lifeline
for communities where water
is not fit to drink.
Like Flint, Michigan, for example.
There, lead pipes poisoned the water,
sickening many
who drank it or bathed in it.
Luckily water can be bottled.
But some things can't.
Like Mari Copeny,
who, at eight years old, wrote a letter to
President Obama asking for his help.
He flew to Flint to meet with Mari.
But she didn't stop there.
She raised funds
for bottled water,
kids' backpacks, and movie tickets.
If we could bottle Mari's courage,
commitment, and compassion,
Flint would have clean water,
justice would flow like a river,
and no one would thirst.

Mari Copeny became an activist at age eight because her life depended on it. In 2014 the town of Flint, Michigan, began to get its water from a new and cheaper source. Treated improperly, the Flint River water corroded city pipes and became contaminated with lead and other toxins. The stinky brown water caused rashes and other sicknesses. And doctors warned that long-term exposure to lead damages children's brains, blood, digestive systems, kidneys, and more. Years after Mari first opened bottles of water to take a bath and help her family cook, she still speaks out about the importance of safe water as "Little Miss Flint."

In your city or state, who has the power to make things change? Write them a letter and ask for what you need.

ZACH WAHLS: WITH ALL DUE RESPECT

A triolet poem by **Lesléa Newman**

I love my mothers more than words can say.
They love me and they love each other, too.
We're family in each and every way.
I love my mothers more than words can say.
Straight or bi or trans or queer or gay,
all couples have the right to say "I do."
I love my mothers more than words can say.
They love me and they love each other, too.

At nineteen, Zach Wahls spoke before Iowa lawmakers about his experience growing up with two mothers. The speech went viral. Zach had learned in Boy Scouts that if he saw a problem, he needed to act. So he used his internet fame to start Scouts for Equality. The organization led the Boy Scouts of America to end its discriminatory practice of not allowing gay members. In 2019 Zach became an Iowa state lawmaker to continue his work toward equality.

Speak from your heart. Focus your message on your passion, and people will listen.

NZA-ARI KHEPRA: *THE ORANGE TREE*

An elegy poem by Andrea J. Loney

The seed
was Hadiya's smile,
gone far too soon.

The sprout
arose from Nza-Ari's choice
to honor the life of her friend
through compassion in action.

The roots
intertwined her classmates' dreams
of a neighborhood,
city,
state,
and country
free from gun violence.

The fruit
bore the color of a hunter's vest.

The color that shouts:
Protect me!
Don't shoot!
My life matters!

Project Orange Tree
first bloomed at one school
on the South Side of Chicago.
But as more seeds fell,
it spread into an orchard,
across an entire nation
of grieving students,
friends,
families,
and communities,
all shouting:
enough!

When Nza-Ari Khepra was sixteen, her friend Hadiya Pendleton was shot and killed. Working through her grief , Nza-Ari joined friends and neighbors to raise awareness about gun violence in Chicago. They hosted open-mic events, candlelight vigils, and a day of fasting and wearing orange. Nza-Ari's grassroots organizing grew from Project Orange Tree into the national Wear Orange campaign, embraced by celebrities and politicians. Now National Gun Violence Awareness Day happens every June in honor of Hadiya's birthday.

Host a color-themed day at your school or in your community to get people thinking about a cause you care about.

VIRIDIANA SANCHEZ SANTOS: QUINCEAÑERA AT THE CAPITOL (UN BAILE DE MOVIMIENTO)

An onomatopoeic poem by Guadalupe García McCall

*C*lick, click, clash!
Let these heels assert our stance.
We are beautiful! Yes, we are!
We are important! And we belong!

Swish, swish, swoosh—
let our skirts flare up like wings.
We are fearless! Yes, indeed!
We are worthy! And we are strong!

Click, click, clash!
Let our sashes scream and shout.
We have dignity! Yes, we do!
We have courage! And we have pride!

Swish, swish, swoosh—
we crown our heads and hold them high.
This is the dance you cannot have.
This is a dance we will not sit out.

Here, on the steps of this capitol—
this dance belongs to us.

Click, click, clash!
¡No más!

In 2017, Viridiana Sanchez Santos was concerned that part of a new Texas law allowed police to demand immigration papers of anyone. Viri didn't have them. Her fear of deportation turned to action when she realized that police might target brown people. She dug out the dress she had worn for her quinceañera—her fifteenth birthday celebration. Then she rallied fourteen friends and sashayed to the Texas State Capitol in protest. They called their graceful show of power "Quinceañera at the Capitol."

Throw a protest party! Use music, dance, and fun to attract an audience.

ADORA SVITAK: ADULTS CAN LEARN FROM KIDS

A free verse poem by Janet Wong

The best and the brightest adults in the world—
    activists, artists, authors,
    educators, engineers,
    mathematicians, musicians, and scientists—
laughed in disbelief and delight
when Adora Svitak, twelve years old, told them
adults can learn from kids.

It bordered on scolding
when she challenged them to
turn kids into . . .
better adults than you have been.

She seemed so adult already,
someone who had left childhood behind
an old laptop and hundreds of stories ago.

Now we wait and hope
that what she said will come true.
We need you—
the ones who will bring this world forward.

Adora Svitak began writing down her ideas about reading, technology, and the power of youth at age four. At eight she published a book of writing tips and taught her first class. A video of her speech "What Adults Can Learn from Kids" captivated millions of grown-ups nationwide. Hundreds of stories, articles, and speeches later, Adora has been honored by a national group of teachers for her efforts to improve education.

Education changes hearts—even in adults. Research your topic and use what you learned to tell an adult why you are seeking change.

MARLEY DIAS: *ONCE*

A free verse poem by Nikki Grimes

Once a girl named Marley,
hardly older than you,
tired of tripping over the invisible spaces
on her fifth-grade reading list.
Mysteriously missing were
stories starring girls
who looked like her.
"What are you going to do about it?"
asked her mom.
The question swept her out to the sea
of her own imagination.
Riding the waves, she dreamed of schools
with black-girl stories stacked
till they skimmed the sky.
Oh! thought Marley suddenly.
That's what I can do!

Back she swam to the world of now,
heart dancing to the rhythm
of a new idea:
she'd gather a mountain of books
boasting characters
as sun-drenched as she,
for schools and libraries
near and far.
Little by little, Marley Dias
became a literacy star.
Thousands of books later,
her dream is still coming true.

It's your turn now.

Close your eyes. Dream a little.
Imagine what *you* can do!

Marley Dias loved to read and wanted more books featuring girls who look like her. She thought other black girls deserved that, too. So Marley launched the #1000BlackGirlBooks social media campaign with the goal of collecting one thousand books. In the first year, eight thousand books flooded in to her school and to others around the world. Marley speaks all over the country and has a book of her own called *Marley Dias Gets It Done: And So Can You!*

Break big problems into small steps. Ask others to help you take the first step.

MAKE SOME NOISE

A free verse poem by
Keila V. Dawson, Jeanette Bradley, and Lindsay H. Metcalf

Sometimes we see a problem
and our hearts ache,
and we think:
Someone should do *something*.

But who is the *someone*?
And what is the *something*?

These fourteen young Americans
chose to be the *someone*
who spoke up,
stood up,
leaped onstage.

They took the mic—
made small voices BIG—

and did *something*
to change our world.

Each of us can be
the someone
who does something.

We can speak our heartache,
sing our joy, and
share our dreams.

We may be small
but
   we
      can
         ROAR!

Not sure how to start? Ask yourself . . .

What is the problem? Why do I care?
Why are things the way they are?
Who has the power to make change?
Who else cares about this issue?
What adults or groups can support me?
What do I want? When do I want it?
Who am I trying to convince, and what's
the best way to reach them?

POETRY FORMS

Ballad: A poem that tells a story, usually in four-line stanzas (or groupings of lines) using an ABCB rhyme scheme—meaning that the second and fourth lines of each stanza rhyme.

Cinquain: A poem made up of five lines. In some cinquains, like the ones in this book, the first line has two syllables, the second line has four syllables, the third six, the fourth eight, and the fifth line once again has two.

Concrete poem: A poem that is shaped like its topic. The words can fill in or outline a shape.

Elegy: A poem honoring someone who has died. An elegy can use poetic devices such as imagery, a technique of painting a picture with words, as the one in this book does. But it doesn't follow a specific form.

Free verse: This unrestricted style does not need to rhyme or follow a beat pattern.

Onomatopoeic poem: A poem featuring words that mimic or suggest sounds.

Reverso: A poem in which the second half uses the same lines as the first half but in reverse order. The second half may also include different punctuation and capitalization to alter the meaning.

Spoken word poem: A poem that is meant to be performed out loud.

Tanka: A Japanese poetic form made up of five lines. Five syllables are used in the first and third lines, with seven syllables in the other lines. Sometimes several tanka appear in a sequence.

Triolet: An eight-line poem in which the first line is repeated as the fourth and seventh lines and the second line is repeated as the eighth line. The first, third, and fifth lines rhyme, as do the second and sixth lines.

Photo credit: Zoë Gemelli

S. Bear Bergman is the founder and publisher of Flamingo Rampant, which makes positive kids' books centering people with diverse genders and orientations. Like Jazz Jennings, he speaks and writes about being trans. **sbearbergman.com**

Photo credit: Aaron Lemen

Nikki Grimes is a *New York Times* best-selling author and has won many awards, including the Children's Literature Legacy Award. She is the author of *Garvey's Choice* and nineteen of the books in Marley Dias's #1000BlackGirlBooks database. **nikkigrimes.com**

Photo credit: Eric Jenks

Joseph Bruchac has created more than 120 books for children and young adults that reflect his Native American heritage. A longtime activist, he visited schools in Standing Rock just before Jasilyn Charger and other water protectors began their blockade. He also organized a benefit concert for the cause. **josephbruchac.com**

Photo credit: Havar Espedal

Hena Khan is the author of picture books, including *Under My Hijab*, and middle-grade stories, including *Amina's Voice*. Like Ziad Ahmed, she works to break down stereotypes about American Muslims. **henakhan.com**

Andrea J. Loney is the award-winning author of *Double Bass Blues*; *Take a Picture of Me, James VanDerZee!*; and *Bunnybear*. She is a computer science instructor at Los Angeles Trade Technical College. Andrea and Nza-Ari Khepra share a commitment to helping black communities. **andreajloney.com**

Guadalupe García McCall writes multicultural books for young people as a form of activism. She is the author of the award-winning verse novel *Under the Mesquite*. Both she and Viridiana Sanchez Santos were born in Mexico and immigrated to Texas at age six. **guadalupegarciamccall.com**

Lindsay H. Metcalf is a journalist and the author of the nonfiction picture books *Farmers Unite! Planting a Protest for Fair Prices* and *Beatrix Potter, Scientist*. Close family members of Lindsay's have suffered from diabetes, like Noah Barnes does. **lindsayhmetcalf.com**

Fiona Morris is a poet with Down syndrome and the author of *Poetry Tingles the Heart*. Both she and Judy Adams support causes that help others with Down syndrome.

G. Neri is an award-winning author of books for children and young adults, including *Ghetto Cowboy*. He and Levi Draheim share a love and concern for the environment of coastal Florida, where they both live. **gneri.com**

Lesléa Newman is the award-winning author of seventy books, including *Heather Has Two Mommies*, the first picture book to portray a family with two moms in a positive way. Both Lesléa and Zach Wahls have traveled the country speaking out about the rights of LGBTQ families. **lesleakids.com**

Photo credit: Kelly Downs

Traci Sorell is an award-winning author of several picture books, including *We Are Grateful: Otsaliheliga* and *At the Mountain's Base*, and the coauthor of *Indian No More*, a middle-grade novel. As an enrolled Cherokee Nation citizen like Cierra Fields, Traci has advocated for the rights of Native American Nations and their citizens at the White House and US Congress. **tracisorell.com**

Photo credit: Gerald Young

Carole Boston Weatherford is the *New York Times* best-selling and award-winning author of *Moses: When Harriet Tubman Led Her People to Freedom*. She teaches at Fayetteville State University in North Carolina. Her writing has lifted the voices of many civil rights heroes, now including Mari Copeny. **cbweatherford.com**

Photo credit: Kim-Julie Hansen

Charles Waters is a children's poet, actor, and educator and the coauthor of *Dictionary for a Better World: Poems, Quotes, and Anecdotes from A to Z* and *Can I Touch Your Hair? Poems of Race, Mistakes, and Friendship*. Like Samirah Horton (DJ Annie Red), Charles is a proud New Yorker and performs his poetry onstage. **charleswaterspoetry.com**

Photo credit: Emily Vardell

Janet Wong has written thirty books, including *Here We Go: A Poetry Friday Power Book*, co-created with Sylvia Vardell, about kids making an impact in their communities. Janet has been featured on the *Oprah Winfrey Show* and at the White House. She met Adora Svitak after hearing her speak at a literacy conference. Both grew up straddling cultures, with one parent who came to the United States from China. **janetwong.com**

The editors would like to extend our gratitude to the young activists featured in this book. This text is much richer because of their participation—and in some cases their parents' or other proxies' participation—through emails, phone calls, and in-person visits. We are also grateful to Dr. Fabio Rojas, professor of sociology at Indiana University, Bloomington, for sharing his research on social movement strategies with us.

For Quinn and Bennett, who are warming up their voices.—L. H. M.

For my mama, who found her voice and passed me the mic.—K. V. D.

For S., whose questions sparked this book, and for G., who makes her voice heard. And for all of you who are shaping our future.—J. B.

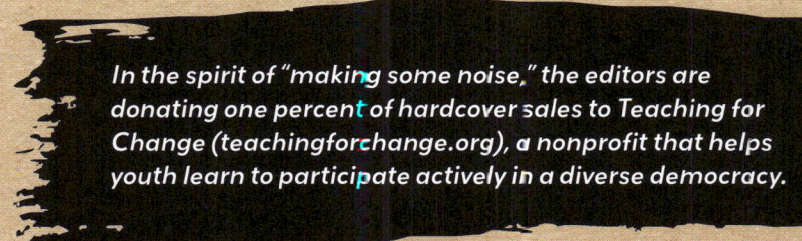

In the spirit of "making some noise," the editors are donating one percent of hardcover sales to Teaching for Change (teachingforchange.org), a nonprofit that helps youth learn to participate actively in a diverse democracy.

Charlesbridge
9 Galen Street
Watertown, MA 02472
(617) 926-0329
www.charlesbridge.com

Library of Congress Cataloging-in-Publication Data
Names: Metcalf, Lindsay H., editor. | Dawson, Keila V., editor. | Bradley, Jeanette, editor, illustrator.
Title: No voice too small : fourteen young Americans making history / edited by Lindsay H. Metcalf, Keila V. Dawson, and Jeanette Bradley; illustrated by Jeanette Bradley.
Description: Watertown, MA: Charlesbridge, [2020] | Summary: Joseph Bruchac, Guadalupe García McCall, and others present poems about young activists who have stepped up to make changes in their community and in the United States.
Identifiers: LCCN 2019014267 (print) | LCCN 2019022336 (ebook) | ISBN 9781623541316 (hardcover) | ISBN 9781632898399 (ebook)
Subjects: LCSH: Social justice—Juvenile poetry. | Social action—Juvenile poetry. | Children's poetry, American. | CYAC: Social action—Juvenile poetry. | American poetry.
Classification: LCC PS595.S75 N6 2020 (print) | LCC PS595.S75 (ebook) | DDC 811/.608—dc23
LC record available at https://lccn.loc.gov/2019014267
LC ebook record available at https://lccn.loc.gov/2019022336

Printed in China • OPIC
The authorized representative in the EU for product safety and compliance is eucomply OÜ Pärnu mnt 139b-14, 11317 Tallinn, Estonia, hello@eucompliancepartner.com, +33757690241
(hc) 10 9 8 7 6 5

Illustrations painted digitally in Procreate for iPad on a digital paper design by Paper Farms
Display type set in Brush Up by PintassilgoPrints
Text type set in Grenadine MVB by Markanna Studios Inc
Color separations by Colourscan Print Co Pte Ltd, Singapore
Production supervision by Brian G. Walker
Designed by Diane M. Earley

"WE CAN'T WAIT FOR THE ADULTS TO FIGHT FOR US. WE HAVE TO FIGHT FOR OURSELVES." —Jasilyn Charger

"I CAN BELIEVE IN MYSELF."
—Noah Barnes

"I DON'T BACK DOWN FROM TOUGH FIGHTS. I'M WILLING TO SPEAK TRUTH TO POWER." —Zach Wahls

"YOU'RE NEVER TOO YOUNG OR TOO SMALL TO CHANGE THE WORLD."
—Mari Copeny